This journal belongs to:

_____.

I STARTED IT ON

this day: _____

in the year: _____

in the city of: _____

when I was in this grade: _____

and was _____ years old.

I COMPLETED IT ON

this day: _____

in the year: _____

in the city of: _____

when I was in this grade: _____

and was _____ years old.

IT WAS GIVEN TO ME BY:

_____

All About ME

A Keepsake Journal For Kids

by LINDA KRANZ

rising moon

Books for Young Readers from Northland Publishing

The text type was set in Journal, Follies, Impact, and Lithos.

The cover illustration and display type were designed by Libba Tracy.

Designed by Rudy J. Ramos.

Edited by Erin Murphy.

Printed in Hong Kong by Wing King Tong Company Limited.

FIRST IMPRESSION 1996

Fourth Printing, January 1998

ISBN 0-87358-658-1

0709/20M/1-98

*For Klaus, the love of my life,
and for Jessica and Nikolaus, my inspiration.*

*And for every child:
Follow your heart and reach for your dreams!*

A Note About this Journal

When I gave birth to Jessica, my first child, one of the most meaningful gifts I received was a calendar called *Baby's First Year*. I began to fill up the pages, looking forward to each new entry. Then, in what seemed like the blink of an eye, Jessica turned one. Writing about her and our family had become such a habit that I had to go out and buy a new, "generic" calendar for her second year. Three years later, just before my son, Nikolaus, was born, I had his calendar already started. Our children grew up watching me write and record our daily lives.

A few years ago I came across a diary that I had kept as a teenager. Jessica was intrigued by what interested me when I was young and she, too, wanted to start keeping a journal. Giving a child a journal and asking her to fill up those blank white pages was a struggle, so I suggested some "thought-starters." That is when her ideas began to flow with ease. Soon after I saw how much she enjoyed expressing herself, I decided to ask Nikolaus questions and record his thoughts, since he was too young to write in his own journal. He, of course, illustrated the pages of his journal in full color.

So you could say that the seed of the idea for *All About Me* has been there for more than thirteen years. The seed began to sprout when I joined the sales department at Northland Publishing; the idea really grew when Northland began publishing children's picture books. When the staff at Northland began to wonder if there were new ways to show the world the artwork from these books, my journal idea finally blossomed into the volume you hold in your hand.

I think we all long to go back to our childhood now and then. I've heard it said that childhood is a forgotten memory, but it doesn't have to be. My family has enjoyed our time together, writing down our thoughts and sharing them with each other. We can relive some of our most happy memories over and over again, just by opening the pages of one of our calendars or journals. Those first "thought-starters" have given us many hours of laughter and a deeper understanding of who we are and how we feel, and have opened up numerous topics of discussion, which is important; as parents, we should stimulate conversations with our children not only to share ideas with them, but to listen to what they have to say.

I feel fortunate that I have had the chance to share these special moments with my family, and I'm excited to share this opportunity with you. May you have happy experiences, as well.

... And a Special Note for Kids

This book is especially for you. Take some time to read through the questions and ideas that I like to call "thought-starters." You can answer the questions more than once, if you like. Always date your entries so you can see how your answers change as you grow.

I hope *All About Me* will inspire you, and that you will look forward to your quiet time alone or with a loved one recording your thoughts.

Now pick up your pen, pencil, or crayon . . . and write!

—LINDA KRANZ

Everyone has a favorite **place**.

Where is **yours?**

What is it **like**?

What do you like to **do** there?

Illustration by Jeanne Arnold from *Carlos and the Cornfield/Carlos y la milpa de maíz*, written by Jan Romero Stevens.

Do you remember your dreams? Draw a picture from one.

Do you
have a
HOBBY?

What is it?

Describe your *favorite* day of **school** this year.

WRITE about anything you want here.

What
makes
you
happy ?

Name *three* things that make you feel important.

Name **something** you have done that makes you **PROUD.**

Illustration by Libba Tracy from *Building a Bridge*, written by Lisa Shook Begaye.

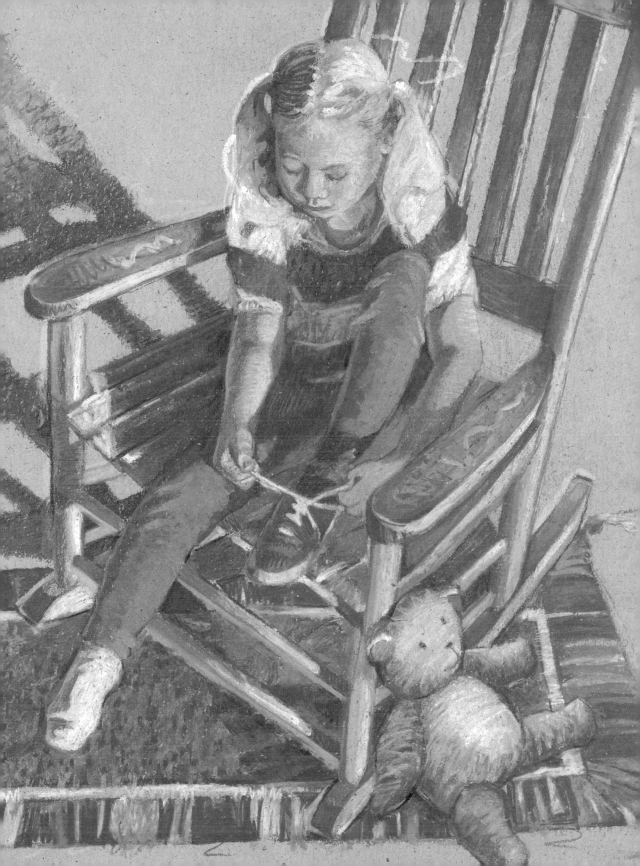

When you **CALL** a friend on the phone, what do you *talk* about?

IF you
could spend
an afternoon
with *someone*
you look
up to,
*who would
it be?*

*What would
you do?*

Illustration by Katalin Olah Ehling from *The Night the Grandfathers Danced*, written by Linda Theresa Raczek.

What do you look like? Draw a picture or place a photograph of yourself here.

What is your favorite subject in school? **WHY?**

What is your least favorite subject? **WHY?**

If you are *stuck* on a problem with your homework, who helps you?

Why do you go to this person?

DRAW
anything you
like here.

Have you ever
taken a **vacation**?

Describe it.

If *you* could visit a **museum**, a **library**, a **sports stadium**, or any **place** you want, where would you visit and why?

What is
your
favorite
HOLIDAY?

How do you
celebrate it?

Sometimes we're afraid to talk about our
most important **DREAMS** because they seem
out of reach.

Is there something you've always wanted to do that
seems **impossible**?

Is there **ONE** little thing you could do that would start
you on the road to your dream?

Use the next two pages to write about it.

Previous illustration by Jim Harris from *The Tortoise and the Jackrabbit*, written by Susan Lowell.

DRAW pictures or place photographs of your best friends here.

about anything
you want here.

Are you an **only** child, or are you the OLDEST child, the **youngest**, or in the **middle?**

What is *special* about being where you are?

Draw a picture or place a photograph of your family here.

Collect happy memories. Do what you think is right. Enjoy today!

Collect happy memories. Do what you think is right. Enjoy today!

Collect happy memories. Do what you think is right. Enjoy today!

Collect happy memories. Do what you think is right. Enjoy today!

Illustration by Libba Tracy from *It Rained on the Desert Today*, written by Ken and Debby Buchanan.

When you lie in your bed at night, just before you drift off to **SLEEP**, what do you *think* about?

What do you think are the three main **problems** in the world?

What would *you* do to change them?

What hurts
your *feelings*?

When you are **SICK**,
what makes you
feel better?

WRITE about anything you want here.

What is something **special** and different about *you*?

What is the best thing about being a **kid**?

Illustration by Libba Tracy from *Building a Bridge*, written by Lisa Shook Begaye.

What time does *school* **START** each morning?

How do you get to school and back *home*?

What do you do **after** school?

IF you could schedule your own school day, what would it be like?

If you could be called by any **name** other than the one you have, what name would you *choose* for yourself and **why**?

 **DRAW**

the floor plan of your house here.
Make notes about things only you would know.

What **movie** could you watch again and again? *Why?*

Name some of your other favorite movies.

What time
do you go
to **BED**?

Who **tucks**
you in?

Do you have
a *special*
routine that
you follow?

DESCRIBE IT.

If you have
trouble
sleeping, what
helps you
fall asleep?

Illustration by Joyce Rossi from *The Gullywasher*, written by Joyce Rossi.

If you could
visit the
MOUNTAINS,
the desert,
or the
seashore,
which would
you choose
and why?

Write down five to ten words that describe your *mom*. Do the same for your **dad**.

Ask *your* parents what they are **PROUD** of.

Write the answer here.

DRAW anything you like here.

Illustration by Redwing T. Nez, from *Forbidden Talent*, story by Redwing T. Nez as told to Kathryn Wilder.

How did
your parents
react
when you
brought home
your last
report card?

What do you
think it is
like to be a
parent?

Have you ever seen **snow**?
If so, draw a memory from
PLAYING in it.
If not, draw what you
imagine snow would be like.

WRITE
*about anything
you want here.*

What do you like to eat for **breakfast**? For LUNCH? For **snacks**? For **DINNER**?

The **NEXT** time you go to the grocery store with your mom or dad, *write* down the prices of six things they put in the shopping cart, **like** bread, milk, or cereal.

Write those prices here with today's **date**.

Illustration by Katalin Olah Ehling from *The Night the Grandfathers Danced*, written by Linda Theresa Raczek.

Who can you **TRUST** with your secrets?

If someone gave you a **million** dollars, what would you do with it?

How does your answer *change* when you think about it for a little longer?

Where does your **dad** work?

What does he do?

Where does your **mom** work?

What does she do?

Do you have a friend or relative you write **letters** *to?*

Who?

What do you **write** *about?*

_____

_____

_____

_____

_____

_____

_____

_____

_____

_____

_____

_____

_____

_____

_____

_____

_____

_____

_____

_____

_____

DRAW anything you like here.

What have
you learned
about being
a friend?

What is a **promise** you have made?

Did you **keep** it?

Describe your *saddest* day.

Illustration by Michael Lacapa from *Less Than Half, More Than Whole*, by Kathleen and Michael Lacapa.

Trace around your hand and color it. Write today's date by it.

Describe your
favorite **book**.

Why do
you like it?

List a few
more books
you like.

What signs
do you
notice
when the
seasons are
about to
change?

WINTER?
Spring?
summer?
FALL?

Illustration by Libba Tracy from *It Rained on the Desert Today*, written by Ken and Debby Buchanan.

What are
your chores
around the
house?

Do you get
an allowance?
How much?

What do
you like to
do on
weekends
and on
**SCHOOL
VACATIONS**?

Have you ever
done something
nice for someone?

Describe it.

Write about an
interesting **place**
you have *visited*.

Parents
are like
teachers.

Write down
five things
that your
parents
have taught
you.

Write five
to ten
words that
describe your
grandparents
or other
relatives.

Listening to your favorite music makes you feel . . .

What makes you **angry**?

What do you do to let your anger out?

Describe your **bedroom.**

Do you share a room or do you have it all to *yourself*?

What do
you like to
daydream
about?

Illustration by Kenneth J. Spengler from *How Jackrabbit Got
His Very Long Ears*, written by Heather Irbinskas.

Write about something you **learned** recently.

Describe how it makes you feel to learn **new** things.

Do you collect something? Draw a picture or place a photograph of your collection here.

Laugh out loud. Do something nice for someone. Never give up.

Laugh out loud. Do something nice for someone. Never give up.

Laugh out loud. Do something nice for someone. Never give up.

Laugh out loud. Do something nice for someone. Never give up.

Do you have
a **PET**?

If so, what
do you like
most about
him or her?

If not, what
would your
perfect
pet be like?

DRAW *your pet, or draw the pet you would like to have.*

Describe a **happy** memory you have of your grandparents.

What do you
want to **be**
when you
grow up?

Do you have a *favorite* song?

Write the words here. If you like, make up your own words for a **new** verse of the song.

Illustration by Jim Harris from *The Three Little Javelinas*, written by Susan Lowell.

What is your favorite **toy**, game, or stuffed animal?

Did your
mom and dad
have *special*
toys when
they were
kids?

*What were
they?*

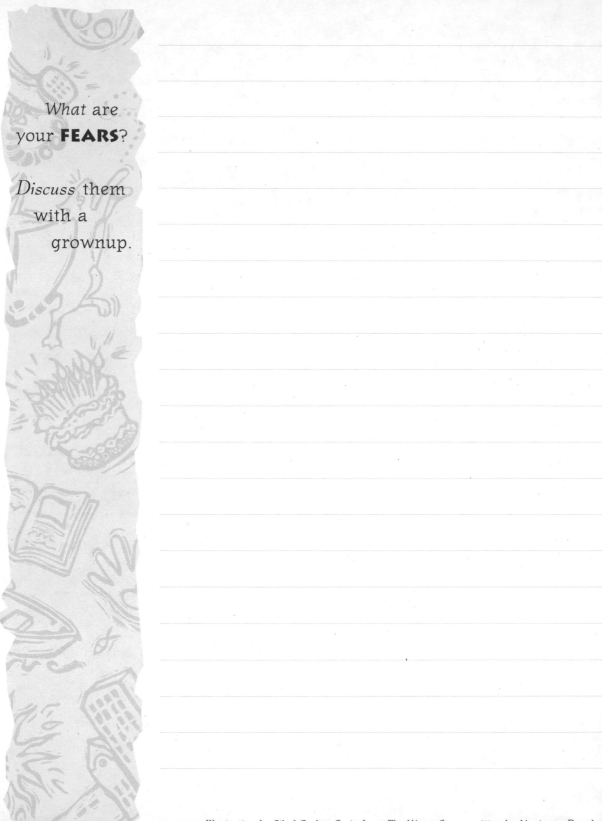

What are
your **FEARS**?

Discuss them
with a
grownup.

Illustration by Sibyl Graber Gerig from *The Worry Stone*, written by Marianna Dengler.

How do you know that someone truly **loves** you even if they don't *say* it?

What type
of **student**
would you
like to teach?

IS there a
teacher who
has made a
DIFFERENCE
to you?

Why is **he** or
she special?

What do you **LIKE** or **DISLIKE** about your neighborhood?

DRAW *your neighborhood here.*

What is the
best **gift**
that you
have received?

Why is it
your *favorite*?

What do you
like to do
together with
your whole
family?

Draw a picture of what you imagine it looks like on the moon.

Illustration by Walter Porter from *The Same Sun Was in the Sky*, by Denise Webb.

How do you **keep** busy on **long** car trips?

Ask your
mom or dad
what they
used to do
for **fun**
when they
were your
AGE.

Ask a
grandparent
what it was
like when he
or she was
a kid.

Write the
answer
here.

What do you
think the
FUTURE
will be like?

What was
your day
like **TODAY**?

How did your
mom and
dad meet?

WRITE
about anything
you want here.

What are the
names of
your best
friends?

What do
you have
in common?

How are you
DIFFERENT?

Ask your parents what **you** were like when you were **little**, or look at old pictures or movies of you. How have you **CHANGED**?

Illustration by Libba Tracy from *It Rained on the Desert Today*, written by Ken and Debby Buchanan.

What qualities
do you **look**
for in a
friend?

Where were you **BORN**?

How many places have you *lived* in?

Where were
your **parents**
born?

How many
places have
they lived in?

Describe your *happiest* day.

Illustration by Joyce Rossi from *The Gullywasher*, written by Joyce Rossi.

IS there someone you know whose *smile* makes you feel good?

Who?

If you had

THREE WISHES,

what would
they be?